dreamers

T0108088

THE BOY WHO WANTED TO FLY

This book belongs to

35
INDIA

Celebrating 35 Years of
Penguin Random House India

Read more in the Dreamers series by Lavanya Karthik

THE BOY WHO WANTED TO FLY

J.R.D. TATA

Written and illustrated by
LAVANYA KARTHIK

duckbill

An imprint of Penguin Random House

For you, with dreams as big as the sky.

DUCKBILL BOOKS

USA | Canada | UK | Ireland | Australia
New Zealand | India | South Africa | China

Duckbill Books is part of the Penguin Random House group of companies
whose addresses can be found at global.penguinrandomhouse.com

Published by Penguin Random House India Pvt. Ltd
4th Floor, Capital Tower 1, MG Road,
Gurugram 122 002, Haryana, India

Penguin
Random House
India

First published in Duckbill Books by
Penguin Random House India 2023

ISBN 9780143461555

Typeset in Georgia by DiTech Publishing Services Pvt. Ltd
Printed at Aarvee Promotions, India

www.penguin.co.in

This is the story of a boy who found his future in the clouds. He was J.R.D. Tata, renowned the world over for his contributions to business, philanthropy and aviation.

But before he became an icon of Indian industry, he was a boy called Jeh seeking his place in the world.

This is his story.

Jeh is a child of two worlds.

There is one that is Indian, like Papa. And the other that is French, like Mama.

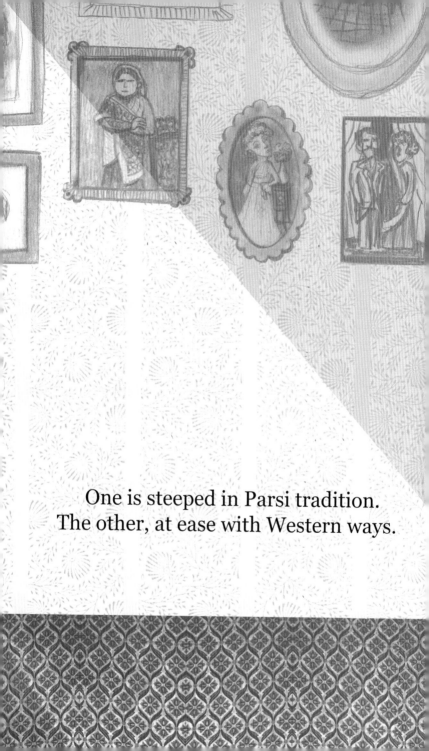

One is steeped in Parsi tradition.
The other, at ease with Western ways.

Life is a constant move between schools, homes and countries, as the family business grows.

Where does Jeh belong?

He is teased for being Indian at the school he attends in Paris.

He is mocked for sounding French at the school in Bombay.

He knows he must follow in Papa's footsteps, yet he dreams of a life filled with adventure.

Where will Jeh belong?

On a summer day, by the sea in France, he watches in awe as the famous aviator Adolphe Pegoud swoops and glides through the clouds. Crowds gasp and cheer as he loops the loop.

Jeh's heart soars with the metal bird flying high over his head.

'I will fly too!' he tells Mama as she tucks him into bed. 'I want to do all the tricks Pegoud did!'

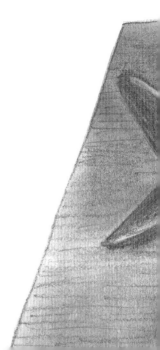

The year Jeh turns ten, war rages across Europe.

Enemy aircraft fly over Paris at night, dropping deadly bombs on its people.

On one such night, Mama hurries the rest of the family to the safety of the cellar. But Jeh wants to see more and he creeps up to the terrace.

Alone in the darkness, Jeh watches as the giant aircraft spreads terror over Paris. And he watches as the city fights back.

'I will fly too!' Jeh tells Mama,
when she leads him down
to safety. 'I will be a pilot and
drop bombs over enemy lines!'

A year after the War ends, Jeh lives his dream at last.

In a fairground outside Paris, Jeh meets a pilot offering rides in his biplane.

'Are you brave enough, young man?' the man asks.

Jeh is so excited, he cannot speak. Then Mama nudges him forward.

The earth falls away under him. The sky reaches out to grab him.

I'm like that daredevil Pegoud! he thinks. *I'm like those zeppelin pilots . . .*

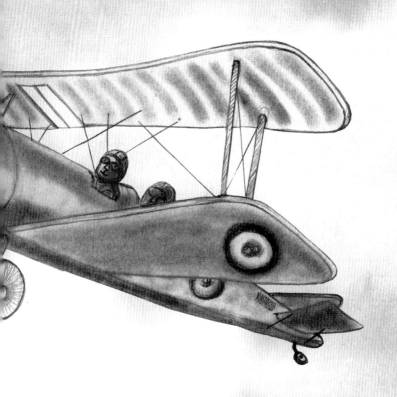

but is he?

Far below him, growing ever smaller, are all the worlds he lives between.

Worlds that seemed so far apart, drawing closer together.

Worlds old and new, growing and changing, just like he is.

'I will fly too,' Jeh tells Mama as they walk home from the fairground.

'To do tricks?' she asks, smiling. 'Or to drop bombs over enemy lines?'

To connect worlds, he thinks.

Among the clouds—that's where
Jeh belongs.

What is . . .

A biplane

A light airplane with two pairs of wings and an engine that could be controlled in the air by a pilot. The first successful flight was achieved in 1903 by the Wright brothers, just a year before Jeh was born.

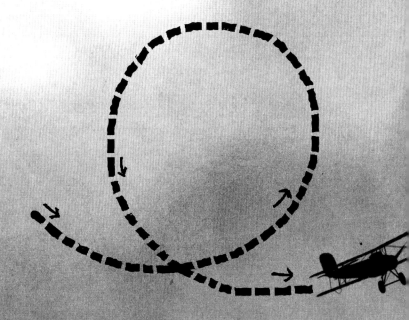

A zeppelin

An early aircraft made of fabric over a metal frame, and filled with hydrogen bags to make it float. They were developed in Germany and were flown at night over enemy lines.

Loop the loop

A dangerous stunt, where the airplane is made to fly in a vertical circle in the air. Pegoud, the famous French pilot, was among the first to accomplish this feat.

Jehangir Ratanji Dadabhoy Tata (29 July 1904–29 November 1993) was one of the world's leading industrialists. He founded many industries and institutes of research and learning, and donated generously to social welfare. He also helped make worker welfare an integral part of the country's legal framework.

In 1929, J.R.D. Tata became India's first licensed pilot and founded the nation's first commercial airline, Tata Airlines (now Air India), in 1932. He flew

its first single-engine aircraft carrying mail from Karachi to Mumbai and continuing to Chennai. He is often called the Father of Indian Civil Aviation.

J.R.D. Tata received many awards in his lifetime, including the Padma Vibhushan, the Bharat Ratna and the French Legion of Honour. He was given the gold air medal of the Federation Aeronautique Internationale. He was also made an honorary Air Vice Marshal in the Indian Air Force, and the honorary Air Commodore of India for his contributions to aviation.

The illustrations in this book are inspired by the art of Pestonji Bomanji (1851–1938), renowned for his portraits of the Parsi community.

Lavanya Karthik is an author by day, a cookie monster by teatime and fast asleep by nine every night. She lives in Mumbai, where she writes, draws, eats a lot of chocolate and takes a lot of naps.